COLONIALISM AND IMPERIALIST'S NEW ARRANGEMENT

THE GOLD GATES IN THIRD WORLD

A BOOK BY
CALEB MAINA IDI

@AMAZON.COM | NOVELUP

COLONIALISM AND IMPERIALIST'S NEW ARRANGEMENT

The Gold Gates in Third World

<u>Table of Contents:</u>

Introduction

Colonialism and imperialism are concepts that have been at the forefront of global history for centuries. They represent a phenomenon where one country or group of countries seeks to dominate and exploit another. While colonialism and imperialism are often used interchangeably, they refer to two different forms of domination. Colonialism refers to the process of establishing and maintaining political control over a foreign territory, while imperialism is the process of extending a country's power and influence through various means, including economic, political, and military.

The historical context of colonialism and imperialism is rooted in the expansionist ambitions of European powers during the 16th century. European powers sought to expand their territories and increase their wealth by exploiting the resources of the new world, which they discovered in the Americas, Africa, and Asia. Colonialism and imperialism were key to the success of European powers in this endeavor. European countries established colonies in various parts of the world, which provided them with access to raw materials and cheap labor.

However, colonialism and imperialism had far-reaching consequences for the countries and people who were colonized. The exploitation of resources and people led to the economic and social underdevelopment of colonized countries, while their cultural and political systems were disrupted and destroyed. The legacy of colonialism and imperialism continues to shape the global political and economic landscape today, as former colonies continue to struggle with the legacy of exploitation and domination.

In this essay, I will provide an overview of colonialism and imperialism and how they impacted the world. I will also discuss the new arrangements that emerged as a result of the decline of colonialism and imperialism, and their impact on global politics and economics.

Colonialism

Colonialism refers to the process of establishing and maintaining political control over a foreign territory. The colonizer exercises political, economic, and cultural control over the colony. Colonialism was a key feature of European expansionism during the 16th century. European powers established colonies in the Americas, Africa, and Asia, which they used as sources of raw materials, labor, and markets for their products.

Colonialism was justified on the basis of cultural, racial, and religious superiority. European powers believed that they had a duty to bring civilization and Christianity to the 'uncivilized' people of the world. This belief was used to justify the exploitation and domination of colonized peoples, who were treated as inferior and subjected to forced labor, land expropriation, and other forms of oppression.

The impact of colonialism on the colonized was profound. The exploitation of resources and people led to economic and social underdevelopment. Colonized countries were used as sources of raw materials, which were exported to Europe and processed into finished products. This resulted in the underdevelopment of local industries, which were unable to compete with European industries. As a result, colonized countries became dependent on imports from Europe, which further contributed to their economic underdevelopment.

Colonialism also had a profound impact on the social and cultural systems of colonized countries. European powers imposed their cultural and religious beliefs on the colonized peoples, often by force. This led to the destruction of local cultures and the suppression of local languages, customs, and traditions. In addition, the political systems of colonized countries were disrupted, as European powers established authoritarian regimes that served their interests.

The legacy of colonialism continues to shape the global political and economic landscape today. Many former colonies continue to struggle with the legacy of exploitation and domination. They are burdened with debt and are unable to compete in the global market. As a result, they remain economically underdeveloped and dependent on foreign aid.

Imperialism

Imperialism is the process of extending a country's power and influence through various means, including economic, political, and military. Imperialism was a key feature of European expansionism during the 19th and early 20th centuries, when European powers sought to expand their territories and increase their wealth by dominating other countries.

Imperialism was driven by a number of factors, including economic, political, and strategic considerations. European powers sought to gain access to new markets for their products, as well as sources of raw materials and cheap labor. In addition, they sought to extend their political influence and control over other countries, in order to secure their strategic interests and maintain their global power.

The impact of imperialism was similar to that of colonialism, although it took different forms. Imperial powers exercised economic, political, and military control over the countries they dominated, and used their power to exploit resources and people. They established trade networks and created economic dependencies, which further reinforced their dominance. Imperial powers also established puppet governments and supported authoritarian regimes that served their interests, often at the expense of local populations.

The legacy of imperialism is still felt today in many parts of the world. Former imperial powers continue to exercise influence and control over former colonies, often through economic and political means. Many countries continue to struggle with the economic and political legacies of imperialism, and are unable to break free from the patterns of dependency and exploitation that were established during the colonial era.

New Arrangements

The decline of colonialism and imperialism has led to the emergence of new arrangements in global politics and economics. In the post-colonial era, many countries have sought to establish new relationships with former colonizers and to assert their independence and sovereignty.

One of the most significant developments in this regard has been the emergence of regional organizations, which seek to promote cooperation and integration among formerly colonized countries. Examples of such organizations include the African Union, the Association of Southeast Asian Nations (ASEAN), and the Caribbean Community (CARICOM).

Regional organizations have played an important role in promoting economic development and political stability in formerly colonized countries. They have facilitated trade and investment, and have helped to reduce economic dependence on former colonizers. They have also provided a platform for political cooperation and the resolution of regional conflicts.

Another important development in the post-colonial era has been the rise of nationalist movements and the assertion of national identity. Many formerly colonized countries have sought to reclaim their cultural and political heritage, and to assert their independence and sovereignty. This has led to the development of new cultural and political movements, which seek to promote national identity and to challenge the legacy of colonialism and imperialism.

At the same time, globalization has emerged as a powerful force in shaping the global economy. Globalization refers to the increasing interconnectedness of the world economy, as a result of advances in technology and communication. Globalization has led to the expansion of trade and investment, and has created new opportunities for economic growth and development.

However, globalization has also created new forms of economic dependency and inequality. Many formerly colonized countries continue to struggle with the legacy of exploitation and underdevelopment, and are unable to compete in the global market. Globalization has also created new challenges for national sovereignty, as global institutions and multinational corporations exercise increasing power and influence over national governments.

Colonialism and imperialism were key features of European expansionism during the 16th and 19th centuries. They represented a process of domination and exploitation, which had profound social, cultural, and economic consequences for the countries and peoples that were colonized. The legacy of colonialism and imperialism continues to shape the global political and economic landscape today, as former colonies struggle with the legacy of exploitation and underdevelopment.

The decline of colonialism and imperialism has led to the emergence of new arrangements in global politics and economics. Regional organizations and nationalist movements have emerged as important forces in promoting economic development and political stability in formerly colonized countries. At the same time, globalization has created new challenges for national sovereignty and has reinforced patterns of economic dependency and inequality.

Moving forward, it is important to acknowledge the historical legacy of colonialism and imperialism and to work towards addressing its ongoing effects. This requires a commitment to promoting economic development and political stability in formerly colonized countries, as well as a recognition of the need for greater global cooperation and solidarity.

It is also important to recognize the role that individual nations and global institutions can play in promoting social justice and equity. By working together to address the challenges of inequality, economic underdevelopment, and political instability, it is possible to build a more just and equitable global community.

Overall, the legacy of colonialism and imperialism highlights the importance of understanding the complex and interconnected nature of global politics and economics. By recognizing the historical roots of current challenges and working towards new solutions, it is possible to build a more just and equitable future for all.

Definition of Colonialism

Colonialism refers to the practice of a powerful country or group of countries establishing and maintaining political, economic, and cultural control over a weaker country or region. This usually involves the colonization of land, the subjugation of people, and the exploitation of resources. The goal of colonialism is usually to extract wealth and resources from the colonized area for the benefit of the colonizing power.

Colonialism can take many forms. In some cases, the colonizing power establishes direct political control over the colony, through the use of military force or political manipulation. In other cases, the colonizing power may establish indirect control, through the use of local leaders or administrators who are sympathetic to the colonizing power's interests.

Colonialism has a long history, dating back to ancient empires such as the Roman and Persian empires. However, the modern era of colonialism began in the 16th century, with the rise of European empires such as Spain, Portugal, and the Netherlands. These empires established colonies in the Americas, Africa, and Asia, and used their superior military technology and economic power to dominate and exploit the people and resources of these regions.

The effects of colonialism on the colonized people and societies were often devastating. Colonization often involved the forced displacement of indigenous peoples, the destruction of traditional cultures and social structures, and the imposition of European values and institutions. Many colonies were also used as sources of cheap labor for the colonizing power's industries, leading to economic exploitation and underdevelopment.

Definition of Imperialism

Imperialism, like colonialism, involves the domination of one society or culture by another. However, imperialism refers specifically to the practice of expanding a country's power and influence through territorial conquest, rather than through direct political or economic control.

Imperialism can take many forms, including military conquest, economic influence, and cultural influence. Imperial powers often seek to expand their territories and spheres of influence through military force, either through the conquest of new territories or the subjugation of weaker countries. They may also use economic power to exert control over other countries, through the use of trade agreements, debt financing, and other economic policies. Finally, they may use cultural influence to spread their values and beliefs to other societies, through the use of media, education, and other forms of soft power.

The origins of imperialism can be traced back to the ancient empires of the Middle East, such as the Assyrian and Persian empires. However, the modern era of imperialism began in the late 19th century, with the rise of European powers such as Great Britain, France, and Germany. These powers competed for control over colonies and territories in Africa, Asia, and the Americas, in what became known as the "Scramble for Africa" and the "New Imperialism."

The effects of imperialism were often similar to those of colonialism, in that they involved the domination and exploitation of weaker societies by stronger ones. However, imperialism often had a more direct and immediate impact on the people and societies being colonized, since it involved the imposition of new political structures, economic policies, and cultural values.

Differences between Colonialism and Imperialism

While colonialism and imperialism are often used interchangeably, there are some key differences between the two concepts. First, colonialism involves the direct or indirect political and economic control of a weaker society by a stronger one, while imperialism involves the expansion of a country's

territory and power through territorial conquest or influence.

Second, colonialism often involves the establishment of colonies, with settlers from the colonizing power living in the colonized area, while imperialism may or may not involve the establishment of new colonies.

Third, colonialism usually involves the exploitation of resources and labor from the colonized area for the benefit of the colonizing power, while imperialism may involve more diverse objectives, such as securing strategic resources, establishing political influence, or expanding cultural influence.

Fourth, colonialism often involves the imposition of new political and social structures on the colonized people, while imperialism may involve more indirect forms of influence, such as economic policies or cultural influence.

Historical Examples of Colonialism

There have been many examples of colonialism throughout history, but perhaps the most well-known examples are those of European colonialism in the Americas, Africa, and Asia during the modern era.

In the Americas, European colonial powers such as Spain, Portugal, France, and England established colonies in the 16th and 17th centuries. These colonies were often used as sources of raw materials and cheap labor for the colonizing power's industries. They were also used as outlets for the colonizing power's surplus population, with settlers from Europe establishing permanent settlements in the new world. The colonizing powers imposed their political and social structures on the indigenous peoples of the Americas, often leading to the displacement, enslavement, and genocide of these peoples.

In Africa, European colonial powers began to establish colonies in the late 19th century, in what became known as the "Scramble for Africa." European powers such as Great Britain, France, Germany, and Belgium carved up the continent into colonies, using their military and economic power to subjugate the local populations. Many African societies were forced into producing cash crops for the colonizing powers, leading to economic exploitation and underdevelopment. The colonizing powers also imposed their political structures on the African societies, often leading to the suppression of indigenous cultures and traditions.

In Asia, European colonial powers such as Great Britain, France, and the Netherlands established colonies in the 17th and 18th centuries. These colonies were often used as trading posts and sources of raw materials for the colonizing powers. The colonizing powers imposed their political structures on the Asian societies, often leading to the suppression of indigenous cultures and traditions.

Historical Examples of Imperialism

Imperialism has also been a common practice throughout history, with many empires seeking to expand their territories and influence through military conquest, economic power, and cultural influence.

One of the most well-known examples of imperialism is that of the Roman Empire. The Romans conquered and annexed territories throughout the Mediterranean and Europe, using their military power to establish a vast empire that lasted for centuries. The Romans also used their economic and cultural influence to spread their values and beliefs to other societies, such as Latin language and law.

In the 19th century, European powers such as Great Britain, France, and Germany engaged in a new era of imperialism, known as the "New Imperialism." These powers sought to expand their territories and influence through military conquest and economic influence, particularly in Africa and Asia. The

British Empire, for example, controlled one-quarter of the world's land surface and population, using its military and economic power to dominate and exploit the people and resources of its colonies.

In the 20th century, the United States also engaged in imperialism, particularly in Latin America and the Pacific. The U.S. used its economic and military power to establish political and economic influence over these regions, often to the detriment of the local populations.

Effects of Colonialism and Imperialism

The effects of colonialism and imperialism have been profound and long-lasting, shaping the political, economic, and cultural landscapes of many societies

Political Effects

One of the most significant effects of colonialism and imperialism has been the imposition of new political structures on the colonized societies. European powers often established colonial administrations that were designed to serve the interests of the colonizing power, rather than those of the colonized people. These administrations often replaced traditional forms of governance, such as tribal or clan-based systems, with centralized systems of government that were more amenable to colonial control.

This had a profound impact on the political development of these societies, often leading to instability and conflict. The imposition of colonial rule also had a profound impact on the national identity of many colonized peoples, leading to a sense of alienation and detachment from their cultural roots.

Economic Effects

The economic effects of colonialism and imperialism have also been significant. European powers often established colonial economies that were designed to serve the interests of the colonizing power, rather than those of the colonized people. This often led to the exploitation of natural resources and the use of forced labor to produce raw materials for export to the colonizing power.

This had a profound impact on the economic development of many colonized societies, often leading to underdevelopment and poverty. The exploitation of natural resources also had a significant impact on the environment, leading to deforestation, soil erosion, and other forms of environmental degradation.

Cultural Effects

The cultural effects of colonialism and imperialism have also been significant. European powers often sought to impose their cultural values and beliefs on the colonized people, often leading to the suppression of indigenous cultures and traditions. This had a profound impact on the social development of many colonized societies, often leading to a loss of cultural identity and a sense of cultural alienation.

Resistance to Colonialism and Imperialism

Despite the many negative effects of colonialism and imperialism, many colonized peoples resisted the imposition of colonial rule and fought for their independence. These struggles often took the form of armed resistance, as well as political and cultural resistance.

One of the most well-known examples of armed resistance to colonialism was the Algerian War of Independence, which lasted from 1954 to 1962. The Algerian National Liberation Front (FLN) waged a guerrilla war against French colonial rule, eventually forcing the French to withdraw from Algeria.

Another example of armed resistance to colonialism was the Mau Mau rebellion in Kenya, which lasted from 1952 to 1960. The Mau Mau rebels fought against British colonial rule, using guerrilla tactics to attack colonial officials and their supporters.

Political and cultural resistance to colonialism also took many forms. In India, for example, Mahatma Gandhi led a nonviolent campaign for independence from British colonial rule, using tactics such as civil disobedience and boycotts of British goods. In Africa, many nationalist leaders emerged in the early 20th century, advocating for the independence of their countries from European colonial rule.

In conclusion, colonialism and imperialism are two related but distinct practices that have had a profound impact on the political, economic, and cultural landscapes of many societies throughout history. While colonialism often involves the establishment of colonies and the direct exploitation of resources and labor from the colonized people, imperialism may involve more diverse objectives, such as securing strategic resources, establishing political influence, or expanding cultural influence. The effects of colonialism and imperialism have been profound and long-lasting, shaping the development of many societies and leading to a variety of political, economic, and cultural outcomes. Despite the many negative effects of these practices, many colonized peoples have resisted them and fought for their independence, leading to the emergence of new nations and the establishment of new political and social structures.

Chapter II
Impacts of colonialism

Colonialism refers to the practice of establishing and maintaining political and economic control over a foreign territory and its people. The impact of colonialism is felt even today, years after the colonial powers withdrew from their colonies. In this essay, we will explore the various impacts of colonialism, including its economic, social, and political effects.

Economic Impacts of Colonialism:

One of the most significant impacts of colonialism was on the economies of colonized countries. Colonizers exploited the natural resources of the colonies, leading to the depletion of these resources. They imposed taxes on the people, which led to impoverishment and a loss of economic independence. Colonizers also established trade monopolies, which forced colonized countries to trade only with them, thereby reducing their ability to develop their economies.

Furthermore, colonialism brought about a restructuring of the economies of the colonized countries. Colonizers introduced cash crops and encouraged the production of raw materials for export. This resulted in the neglect of local industries and the underdevelopment of manufacturing sectors. Consequently, colonized countries became heavily reliant on the export of primary commodities, which made them vulnerable to market fluctuations and price shocks.

Social Impacts of Colonialism:

Colonialism had a profound impact on the social structures of colonized countries. It led to the introduction of new social classes, with the colonizers occupying the top positions, and the colonized people occupying the lower positions. This resulted in the exploitation of the labor of the colonized people, as they were forced to work in harsh conditions in mines, plantations, and factories.

Moreover, colonialism led to the imposition of European cultural and social values on colonized countries. Colonizers forced their language, religion, and customs on the people, resulting in the loss of local culture and traditions. This led to a loss of identity and a sense of inferiority among colonized people, which persists even today.

Political Impacts of Colonialism:

Colonialism also had significant political impacts on colonized countries. Colonizers imposed their political systems on colonized people, leading to the establishment of authoritarian and exploitative governments. This resulted in the denial of political freedoms and human rights to the people.

Furthermore, colonialism created borders that divided communities and ethnic groups. These borders did not take into account the cultural and linguistic affinities of the people and resulted in the creation of artificial states. This led to conflicts and tensions among different groups and communities, which persist even today.

In conclusion, colonialism had far-reaching impacts on the economies, societies, and politics of colonized countries. Its legacy is still felt in many parts of the world today, and it is important to acknowledge and address these impacts to promote social justice and economic development.

Chapter III
New Arrangements of Imperialism

Imperialism refers to the policy or practice of extending a country's power and influence through colonization, use of military force, or other means of economic, political, and cultural domination. Historically, imperialism was closely linked with colonialism, in which a stronger country would establish and maintain colonies in weaker countries or regions. However, with the decline of formal colonialism in the 20th century, imperialism has taken on new forms and arrangements. This essay will explore three of these new arrangements: neocolonialism, economic imperialism, and cultural imperialism.

Neocolonialism

Neocolonialism is a term used to describe a situation in which a country maintains control over another country or region, even after formal independence has been achieved. Neocolonialism is often seen as a continuation of colonialism, albeit in a more subtle and indirect form. Neocolonialism is achieved through a variety of means, including economic, political, and military control.

Economically, neocolonialism is achieved through the domination of the weaker country's economy by the stronger country. This domination can take many forms, including the control of natural resources, the establishment of multinational corporations, and the imposition of structural adjustment programs. In many cases, the weaker country is left with little control over its own economy, and is forced to depend on the stronger country for economic development.

Politically, neocolonialism is achieved through the manipulation of the weaker country's political system. This can take many forms, including the imposition of leaders who are friendly to the stronger country, the provision of military and economic aid to the weaker country, and the establishment of military bases in the weaker country. In many cases, the weaker country is left with little control over its own political system, and is forced to align itself with the interests of the stronger country.

Militarily, neocolonialism is achieved through the use of military force to maintain control over the weaker country. This can take many forms, including the deployment of troops to the weaker country, the establishment of military bases in the weaker country, and the provision of military aid to the weaker country. In many cases, the weaker country is left with little control over its own security, and is forced to rely on the stronger country for protection.

Neocolonialism has been criticized for perpetuating the exploitation of weaker countries by stronger countries, and for inhibiting the development and progress of weaker countries. Critics argue that neocolonialism undermines the sovereignty and independence of weaker countries, and perpetuates a global system of inequality and domination.

Economic Imperialism

Economic imperialism is a term used to describe a situation in which a stronger country dominates the economy of a weaker country through the use of economic power. Economic imperialism is achieved through a variety of means, including the establishment of multinational corporations, the control of natural resources, and the imposition of trade policies.

Multinational corporations play a major role in economic imperialism. These corporations are typically based in stronger countries, and operate in weaker countries through subsidiaries or joint ventures. Multinational corporations often dominate the economy of weaker countries, and can exert significant influence over the political system of these countries. This influence can take many forms, including the provision of economic aid, the establishment of relationships with local elites, and the lobbying of government officials.

The control of natural resources is another key aspect of economic imperialism. Many weaker countries are rich in natural resources such as oil, minerals, and timber. Stronger countries often seek to control these resources, either through direct ownership or through contracts with local companies. The exploitation of these resources can lead to environmental degradation and the displacement of local communities.

Finally, the imposition of trade policies can also contribute to economic imperialism. Stronger countries often use trade policies to gain advantages over weaker countries, such as imposing tariffs and quotas on imports from weaker countries, while promoting their own exports. This can lead to a situation in which weaker countries become dependent on stronger countries for trade, and are unable to develop their own industries and economies.

Critics of economic imperialism argue that it perpetuates global inequality and exploitation. They argue that economic imperialism limits the development and progress of weaker countries, and that it undermines the sovereignty and independence of these countries. They also argue that economic imperialism can lead to environmental degradation, social upheaval, and political instability.

Cultural Imperialism

Cultural imperialism is a term used to describe a situation in which a stronger culture dominates and influences the culture of a weaker culture. Cultural imperialism is achieved through a variety of means, including the media, education, and popular culture.

The media plays a major role in cultural imperialism. Stronger countries often dominate the global media, and use this dominance to promote their own culture and values. This can lead to a situation in which weaker cultures are marginalized or excluded from the global media, and are unable to promote their own cultural values and traditions.

Education is another key aspect of cultural imperialism. Stronger countries often promote their own educational systems and values in weaker countries, often through the establishment of international schools and universities. This can lead to a situation in which weaker cultures are unable to develop their own educational systems and values, and are forced to adopt those of the stronger culture.

Finally, popular culture can also contribute to cultural imperialism. Stronger countries often export their own popular culture, such as music, movies, and television shows, to weaker countries. This can lead to a situation in which weaker cultures are unable to promote their own cultural values and traditions, and are forced to adopt those of the stronger culture.

Critics of cultural imperialism argue that it perpetuates cultural domination and homogenization. They argue that cultural imperialism limits the diversity and richness of global cultures, and that it undermines the autonomy and creativity of weaker cultures. They also argue that cultural imperialism can lead to social and psychological alienation, as weaker cultures are unable to identify with or relate to the dominant culture.

In conclusion, new arrangements of imperialism have emerged in the 21st century, including neocolonialism, economic imperialism, and cultural imperialism. These new arrangements perpetuate global inequality and exploitation, and undermine the sovereignty and independence of weaker countries. They limit the development and progress of weaker countries, and undermine the diversity and richness of global cultures. Addressing these new arrangements of imperialism will require a concerted effort to promote global cooperation and solidarity, and to challenge the dominance and influence of stronger countries. It will also require a commitment to promoting the autonomy and creativity of weaker cultures, and to ensuring that all people have access to the resources and opportunities they need to thrive.

Chapter IV
The Persistence of Colonialism and Imperialism Today

Colonialism and imperialism refer to the domination of one country by another country or group of countries. Historically, these concepts have been associated with the European expansion of the 16th to the 20th centuries, during which time European powers established colonies and territories in Africa, Asia, and the Americas. However, colonialism and imperialism are not simply historical phenomena. They persist in various forms today and continue to shape global power relations.

Contemporary Forms of Colonialism and Imperialism

Economic Imperialism

One of the most prominent contemporary forms of imperialism is economic imperialism. Economic imperialism refers to the economic domination of one country by another country or group of countries. In this form of imperialism, the dominating country controls the economic resources of the dominated country and uses them for its own benefit. Economic imperialism can take many forms, including foreign direct investment, free trade agreements, and debt bondage.

Foreign direct investment (FDI) is one way that economic imperialism is perpetuated. In this form of investment, a company from one country invests in a company or project in another country. The investment can take many forms, including the purchase of shares in a company or the financing of a construction project. In exchange for the investment, the company from the dominating country gains a degree of control over the company or project in the dominated country. This control can include decision-making power, access to resources, and the ability to set prices.

Free trade agreements are another form of economic imperialism. These agreements are designed to promote trade between countries by eliminating tariffs and other trade barriers. However, free trade agreements often benefit the dominant country at the expense of the dominated country. For example, a dominant country may be able to flood the market of a dominated country with cheap imports, which can put local businesses out of business.

Debt bondage is a third form of economic imperialism. In this form of imperialism, a country is forced to take on large amounts of debt from the dominant country or international organizations. The debt can be used to finance development projects, but often comes with conditions attached. These conditions can include policies that benefit the dominant country, such as the privatization of public services or the opening of markets to foreign companies. Debt bondage can be difficult to escape, as the interest on the debt can quickly become unmanageable.

Cultural Imperialism

Another contemporary form of imperialism is cultural imperialism. Cultural imperialism refers to the spread of the dominant culture of one country or group of countries to other countries. This can take many forms, including the dominance of the English language, the spread of Western popular culture, and the imposition of Western values and norms.

The dominance of the English language is one of the most visible forms of cultural imperialism. English is widely spoken around the world and is often used as the language of international business, diplomacy, and education. This gives English-speaking countries a significant advantage in global affairs, as they are able to communicate with other countries more easily than non-English-speaking countries.

The spread of Western popular culture is another form of cultural imperialism. Western popular culture, including music, movies, and television shows, is exported around the world and often displaces local cultural expressions. This can lead to a homogenization of global culture, as Western cultural products become dominant.

The imposition of Western values and norms is a third form of cultural imperialism. Western countries often promote their own values and norms, such as democracy, human rights, and individualism, as universal values that should be adopted by other countries. This can lead to a rejection of local cultural practices and a sense of cultural inferiority.

Neocolonialism

Neocolonialism refers to the continued domination of a country by another country or group of countries, even after the formal end of colonialism. Neocolonialism is often perpetuated through economic, political, and military means.

Economically, neocolonialism can take the form of resource exploitation. Many former colonies are rich in natural resources, such as oil, minerals, and timber. These resources are often owned and controlled by foreign companies, which extract them for their own benefit, without giving back to the local economy. This can lead to a dependency on resource exports and a lack of diversification in the local economy.

Politically, neocolonialism can take the form of interference in the political affairs of a country. Powerful countries may support political leaders who are friendly to their interests, or they may use economic pressure to influence the policies of a country. This can lead to a lack of democracy and a sense of powerlessness among the local population.

Militarily, neocolonialism can take the form of military intervention. Powerful countries may use their military forces to intervene in the affairs of other countries, in order to protect their interests or to promote their values. This can lead to a loss of sovereignty and a sense of vulnerability among the local population.

Resistance to Colonialism and Imperialism

Despite the persistence of colonialism and imperialism, there have been many movements of resistance throughout history. These movements have taken many forms, including armed struggle, civil disobedience, and cultural resistance.

Armed Struggle

Armed struggle has been one of the most visible forms of resistance to colonialism and imperialism. Armed struggle involves the use of violence to achieve political goals. Many independence movements in Africa and Asia were led by armed groups that fought against colonial powers.

One of the most famous examples of armed struggle was the Algerian War of Independence, which lasted from 1954 to 1962. The National Liberation Front (FLN) led an armed struggle against French colonial rule, which eventually led to the independence of Algeria.

Another example of armed struggle was the Cuban Revolution, which lasted from 1953 to 1959. The revolution was led by Fidel Castro and his supporters, who overthrew the Cuban government and established a socialist state.

Civil Disobedience

Civil disobedience is another form of resistance to colonialism and imperialism. Civil disobedience involves the refusal to obey certain laws or rules, in order to bring about political change. Civil disobedience can take many forms, including protests, sit-ins, and boycotts.

One of the most famous examples of civil disobedience was the Indian independence movement led by Mahatma Gandhi. Gandhi and his supporters used nonviolent tactics, such as peaceful protests and civil disobedience, to challenge British rule in India.

Another example of civil disobedience was the American civil rights movement led by Martin Luther King Jr. King and his supporters used nonviolent tactics, such as sit-ins and boycotts, to challenge racial segregation in the United States.

Cultural Resistance

Cultural resistance is another form of resistance to colonialism and imperialism. Cultural resistance involves the use of culture, art, and language to assert cultural identity and challenge dominant cultural norms.

One example of cultural resistance was the Harlem Renaissance, a cultural movement that took place in the United States in the 1920s and 1930s. The Harlem Renaissance was led by African American writers, musicians, and artists, who used their work to challenge stereotypes and assert their cultural identity.

Another example of cultural resistance was the Māori renaissance, a cultural movement that took place in New Zealand in the 1960s and 1970s. The Māori renaissance was led by Māori artists, musicians, and activists, who used their work to assert Māori cultural identity and challenge dominant cultural norms.

Colonialism and imperialism have had a profound and lasting impact on the world. Although formal colonialism has come to an end, neocolonialism persists, perpetuating economic, political, and military domination by powerful countries over weaker ones.

Resistance to colonialism and imperialism has taken many forms throughout history, including armed struggle, civil disobedience, and cultural resistance. These movements have challenged the dominant power structures and asserted the rights and identities of marginalized groups.

Today, it is important to continue to recognize and resist neocolonialism and imperialism in all its forms, and to support movements of resistance around the world. This includes standing in solidarity with Indigenous and marginalized communities, advocating for economic and political justice, and working towards a more equitable and just world for all.

Chapter V
Definition of Third World and Gold

The terms "Third World" and "gold" are not inherently related, but they both have important historical contexts and implications for global power dynamics.

"Third World" originated during the Cold War as a way to categorize countries that were not aligned with either the capitalist First World (led by the United States) or the communist Second World (led by the Soviet Union). The term was used to describe countries that were seen as economically and politically underdeveloped, often former colonies of European powers. Today, the term is considered outdated and politically incorrect, and many prefer to use terms like "developing countries" or "Global South" instead.

Gold, on the other hand, has long been valued for its beauty and rarity, and has been used as a symbol of wealth and power for centuries. The mining and trade of gold has had a significant impact on global history, especially during the colonial era.

Colonialism and the Gold Trade

European powers first began exploring and colonizing the Americas in the late 15th century, and soon discovered vast deposits of gold and silver. The Spanish, in particular, became known for their exploitation of gold mines in South America, using forced labor to extract the precious metal.

The gold trade played a major role in the development of the global economy during the colonial era. Gold was used to finance wars, build empires, and enrich European monarchs and merchants. However, the wealth generated by the gold trade was not evenly distributed, and the exploitation of indigenous peoples and African slaves to extract the gold was brutal and inhumane.

Impact of Colonialism on Third World Countries

The legacy of colonialism and the exploitation of resources like gold has had a lasting impact on many Third World countries. In many cases, colonizers established extractive economies that were designed to benefit the colonizing powers at the expense of the colonized people. These economies often relied on forced labor or cheap wages to extract natural resources like gold, and the profits were exported to Europe or North America.

Today, many Third World countries continue to struggle with poverty, political instability, and inequality as a result of the legacy of colonialism. Some argue that the ongoing exploitation of natural resources by multinational corporations continues to perpetuate these inequalities.

Gold as a Symbol of Wealth and Power

Gold has long been a symbol of wealth and power, and this symbolism is still present today. Gold is used in jewelry and other luxury goods, and is often seen as a safe investment in times of economic uncertainty. However, the association of gold with wealth and power also reflects the historical legacy of colonialism and the exploitation of natural resources.

Exploitation of Gold Mines and Labor

The mining of gold can have devastating environmental and social impacts, especially in developing countries where regulations may be weak or nonexistent. The use of chemicals like mercury and cyanide to extract gold can contaminate water sources and harm wildlife and human health. In addition, the labor practices in many gold mines are exploitative, with low wages and dangerous working conditions.

Efforts to address these issues have included the development of responsible mining standards and the promotion of fair trade gold, which seeks to ensure that gold is mined and traded in a way that respects human rights and the environment.

Overall, the history and symbolism of gold is intertwined with global power dynamics and the legacy of colonialism. The exploitation of natural resources like gold has had lasting impacts on Third World countries, and efforts to address these issues continue today.

Chapter VI
Contemporary Gold Mining Practices

Gold mining has been a significant industry for centuries, and it continues to be so today. However, modern mining practices have evolved significantly since the early days of gold prospecting. In this article, we will explore contemporary gold mining practices, including modern mining techniques and technologies, labor conditions and human rights abuses, and environmental degradation and health risks.

Modern Mining Techniques and Technologies

Modern mining techniques and technologies have transformed the way gold mining is conducted. Some of the most significant developments in modern mining include the following:

Automated drilling: Automated drilling allows for more efficient and accurate drilling, resulting in less waste and more gold extraction.

Sensor technology: Sensor technology can detect the presence of gold deposits more accurately and efficiently than traditional methods.

Remote-controlled vehicles: Remote-controlled vehicles allow for safer and more efficient mining in dangerous or hard-to-reach areas.

Chemical extraction: Chemical extraction methods, such as cyanide leaching, have made it possible to extract gold from low-grade ores and previously unprofitable deposits.

Reclamation technology: Reclamation technology allows for the restoration of mined land, reducing the impact of mining on the environment.

Labor Conditions and Human Rights Abuses

Gold mining has a long history of labor exploitation and human rights abuses. In many parts of the world, miners work in dangerous conditions, with inadequate safety equipment and training. Child labor and forced labor are also common in some countries.

In addition to physical dangers, miners also face significant health risks from exposure to toxic chemicals, such as mercury and cyanide, used in the gold extraction process. These chemicals can cause serious health problems, including neurological damage, kidney damage, and cancer.

Environmental Degradation and Health Risks

Gold mining can have significant environmental impacts, including deforestation, soil erosion, and water pollution. The use of toxic chemicals in the extraction process can also harm local ecosystems and wildlife.

In addition to environmental damage, gold mining can also pose significant health risks to nearby communities. The release of toxic chemicals into the air and water can cause serious health problems, including respiratory problems, skin irritation, and reproductive issues.

Contemporary gold mining practices have come a long way since the early days of gold prospecting. Modern mining techniques and technologies have made gold mining more efficient and profitable, but they have also brought new environmental and health risks. Labor conditions and human rights abuses continue to be a significant problem in some parts of the world, and it is essential to address these issues to ensure that the benefits of gold mining are shared equitably and sustainably.

Chapter VII
Global Gold Markets and Trade

Gold has been a valuable and sought-after commodity throughout human history. Today, gold continues to be a significant part of global trade and investment, with its market valued in the trillions of dollars. In this article, we will explore the role of Europe and America in the gold markets, price fixing and manipulation, and trade relationships with third world countries.

Role of Europe and America in Gold Markets

Europe and America have historically played a significant role in the global gold markets. The United States, in particular, has been a major player in the gold market, with the country holding a large amount of gold reserves. The U.S. gold reserve is the largest in the world, with over 8,000 tons of gold in its vaults. Additionally, many of the largest gold mining companies in the world are based in Europe and the United States.

Europe has also been a major player in the gold market, with London being a key center for gold trading. The London Bullion Market Association (LBMA) sets the global standard for gold trading, and the majority of the world's gold is traded through LBMA members. European countries, such as Switzerland and Germany, have also historically been significant gold traders and refiners.

Price Fixing and Manipulation

Like any commodity, the price of gold is subject to fluctuations based on supply and demand. However, there have been instances of price fixing and manipulation in the gold market. In 2014, several major banks were fined for manipulating the gold market. The banks were accused of rigging the gold price by sharing information about client orders and coordinating their trades. The fines for these actions totaled more than $2.5 billion.

The gold market is also subject to manipulation through the use of derivatives. Derivatives are financial instruments that are used to speculate on the price of gold. They can be used to artificially inflate the price of gold or to suppress it. However, the use of derivatives in the gold market is regulated, and there are measures in place to prevent manipulation.

Trade Relationships with Third World Countries

The gold trade has been an important source of income for many third world countries. These countries are often rich in natural resources, including gold, but lack the infrastructure and resources to fully develop their mining industries. As a result, many third world countries sell their gold to larger, more developed countries.

However, the trade of gold can be problematic, particularly when it involves artisanal and small-scale mining (ASM). ASM is often informal, and the miners may not receive fair prices for their gold. Additionally, ASM can lead to environmental damage and human rights abuses. The use of child labor in ASM is also a significant issue.

To address these problems, there are several initiatives in place to promote responsible gold mining and trade. The Responsible Jewellery Council (RJC) is an organization that promotes responsible mining and supply chains. The RJC sets standards for ethical mining and trade practices and provides certification for responsible mining companies. Other initiatives, such as the Fairtrade Gold program, also promote fair trade practices in the gold industry.

Gold remains an important part of the global economy and trade. Europe and America continue to play a significant role in the gold market, with the United States holding the largest gold reserve in the world and London being a key center for gold trading. However, the gold market is subject to price fixing and manipulation, which can have significant consequences for traders and investors. Additionally, the trade of gold can be problematic, particularly when it involves artisanal and small-scale mining. Initiatives to promote responsible gold mining and trade are necessary to ensure that the gold industry is sustainable and ethical.

Chapter VIII
Resistance and Struggle

Resistance and struggle have been key features of human societies throughout history, as individuals and communities have sought to resist oppression and exploitation and assert their rights and freedoms. In the modern era, resistance movements have taken many forms, from political and social activism to armed struggle and guerrilla warfare. This essay will explore three different aspects of resistance and struggle: Third World resistance movements against gold exploitation, environmental and human rights activism, and government policies and regulations.

Third World Resistance Movements Against Gold Exploitation

Gold mining has been a major driver of economic growth and development in many Third World countries, but it has also been a source of conflict and controversy. In recent years, there has been growing resistance to gold mining in many parts of the world, particularly in regions where indigenous communities and other marginalized groups are most affected by the environmental and social impacts of mining.

One example of such resistance is the struggle of the Yanomami people in Brazil and Venezuela, who have been fighting for decades to protect their ancestral lands from gold mining and other forms of resource extraction. The Yanomami, one of the largest indigenous groups in the Amazon region, have faced widespread violence and displacement as a result of mining activities, as well as the spread of diseases brought by outsiders. Despite facing significant challenges, the Yanomami have continued to resist mining and other forms of encroachment on their lands, working with allies and supporters around the world to raise awareness of their struggle.

Similar resistance movements have emerged in other parts of the world, including Africa and Asia, where local communities and activists have challenged the negative impacts of gold mining on their health, livelihoods, and environment. These movements have often faced significant obstacles, including violence, intimidation, and repression by government and corporate forces, but they have also inspired others to join the struggle for justice and accountability.

Environmental and Human Rights Activism

In recent years, there has been a growing recognition of the linkages between environmental degradation, human rights violations, and social inequality. Activists and organizations around the world have mobilized to challenge these interconnected problems, often working across different issue areas and geographical contexts to build alliances and solidarity.

One example of such activism is the movement for climate justice, which seeks to address the root causes of climate change and its impacts on vulnerable communities, particularly in the Global South. This movement has brought together a diverse range of actors, from indigenous communities and peasant farmers to urban youth and environmental organizations, to demand urgent action on climate change and to challenge the power of fossil fuel companies and other vested interests.

Another example of environmental and human rights activism is the movement for water justice, which seeks to defend the right to clean and accessible water for all people, regardless of their income or social status. This movement has emerged in response to the growing threat of water scarcity and pollution, which is often exacerbated by corporate greed and government corruption. Activists and communities around the world have organized protests, campaigns, and legal actions to challenge the privatization and commodification of water resources and to demand greater accountability and transparency from those who control them.

Government Policies and Regulations

Finally, it is important to consider the role of government policies and regulations in shaping resistance and struggle. While governments can play a positive role in supporting social justice and environmental sustainability, they can also be complicit in the oppression and exploitation of marginalized groups, particularly when they prioritize the interests of corporate elites and other powerful actors over the needs and rights of ordinary people.

One example of this is the ongoing struggle for land reform in many parts of the world, where governments have often failed to address the historical and ongoing injustices of land dispossession and unequal distribution. In countries such as South Africa, Brazil, and the Philippines, social movements and civil society organizations have pushed for more radical and transformative policies to address these issues, including the redistribution of land to those who have been historically excluded or marginalized. However, these movements have often faced resistance and repression from governments and powerful elites who are invested in maintaining the status quo.

Another example of government policies and regulations shaping resistance and struggle is the debate around corporate social responsibility (CSR). While many companies have adopted CSR policies and practices as a way to address environmental and social concerns, critics argue that these efforts are often superficial and do not address the underlying structural issues that perpetuate inequality and exploitation. As such, some activists and organizations have pushed for stronger regulations and accountability measures to ensure that companies are held responsible for their actions and that they do not undermine the rights and well-being of local communities and ecosystems.

In conclusion, resistance and struggle are central features of contemporary social and environmental movements, as individuals and communities seek to challenge oppression and exploitation and build a more just and sustainable world. From Third World resistance movements against gold exploitation to environmental and human rights activism and struggles for government policies and regulations that promote social justice, these movements are diverse, complex, and often challenging. However, they are also essential for building a more equitable and sustainable future for all.

Chapter IX
Case Studies

Case Study 1: Ghana - A History of Gold Mining and Exploitation

Ghana, located in West Africa, has a rich history of gold mining and exploitation dating back to pre-colonial times. The gold-rich land attracted European traders, who sought to establish trade relationships with the local chiefs to obtain gold. The Portuguese were the first to arrive in Ghana in the 15th century, followed by the Dutch, British, and Danes.

During colonial rule, gold mining was industrialized, with the establishment of large-scale mines by British companies, such as Ashanti Goldfields and Gold Coast Company. The British colonial government implemented policies to promote gold mining, which included the introduction of mining legislation, tax incentives, and the creation of the Gold Coast Chamber of Mines.

However, the exploitation of gold resources in Ghana has had significant environmental and social impacts. The use of mercury and cyanide in gold mining has led to widespread environmental pollution, with water bodies being contaminated and farmlands destroyed. The health of miners and nearby communities has also been affected by exposure to toxic chemicals.

Despite these challenges, gold mining remains a vital industry in Ghana's economy, contributing about 5% of the country's GDP and providing employment for thousands of people. The government has implemented measures to regulate and manage the industry, such as the establishment of the Environmental Protection Agency and the Minerals Commission, to enforce environmental and mining laws.

Case Study 2: Colombia - Conflict and Environmental Degradation in the Gold Industry

Colombia is one of the largest gold producers in Latin America, with the metal accounting for a significant portion of the country's exports. However, the gold industry in Colombia is plagued by conflicts and environmental degradation.

Illegal mining operations, often carried out by armed groups, have led to violence and displacement of local communities. These groups use the profits from illegal mining to finance their activities, perpetuating a cycle of violence and instability.

The use of mercury and other toxic chemicals in gold mining has led to widespread environmental pollution, with rivers and soil being contaminated. The health of miners and nearby communities has also been affected by exposure to toxic chemicals.

The Colombian government has implemented measures to regulate the industry and address these challenges, such as the creation of the National Mining Agency and the Ministry of Mines and Energy. The government has also signed agreements with mining companies to promote responsible mining practices and protect the environment.

Case Study 3: South Africa - The Legacy of Apartheid and Gold Mining

South Africa is one of the world's largest gold producers, with the metal accounting for a significant portion of the country's exports. However, the gold mining industry in South Africa has a complicated history, with the legacy of apartheid having a significant impact.

During apartheid, black South Africans were denied access to land and resources, including gold mines.

The gold mining industry was dominated by white-owned companies, who used black labor to extract the gold. The working conditions for black miners were harsh, with long hours, low wages, and poor safety standards.

Since the end of apartheid, the South African government has implemented measures to address the legacy of inequality and promote black ownership of mines. The Mineral and Petroleum Resources Development Act of 2002 requires mining companies to comply with certain black economic empowerment requirements, such as ownership and management by black South Africans.

However, the gold mining industry in South Africa still faces significant challenges, such as declining reserves, increasing labor costs, and ongoing safety concerns. The government and mining companies are working together to address these challenges and ensure the sustainability of the industry.

Chapter X

Slavery in Underdeveloped Nations

Slavery, a practice where people are treated as property and forced to work for little or no pay, has existed throughout human history. Slavery has been a global phenomenon and was prevalent in many underdeveloped nations in the past. In this article, we will provide a brief historical overview of slavery, discuss the forms of slavery in underdeveloped nations, and analyze the impact of slavery on underdeveloped nations.

Historical Overview of Slavery:

Slavery has been recorded throughout history, with evidence of the practice dating back to ancient civilizations such as Egypt, Greece, and Rome. In the 15th century, European countries began colonizing Africa and the Americas and started to use African slaves to work on their plantations. The transatlantic slave trade was established, and millions of Africans were forcibly taken from their homes and sold into slavery. The slave trade continued until the 19th century, when it was abolished in most countries.

Forms of Slavery in Underdeveloped Nations:

Although slavery is now illegal in most countries, it still exists in many underdeveloped nations. The forms of slavery in these nations vary, but some common types include debt bondage, forced labor, and human trafficking.

Debt bondage occurs when people are forced to work to pay off a debt. This practice is prevalent in many countries in South Asia, where people often borrow money from lenders and are forced to work for very little pay to repay the debt. The cycle of debt can be passed down from generation to generation, resulting in families being trapped in a cycle of poverty.

Forced labor is another form of slavery that is widespread in underdeveloped nations. People are often forced to work in harsh conditions, with little or no pay, and no way to leave. This practice is often used in industries such as mining, agriculture, and manufacturing.

Human trafficking is the third form of slavery that is prevalent in underdeveloped nations. People are often kidnapped or tricked into leaving their homes with promises of better jobs or a better life. They are then forced to work as slaves in various industries, including prostitution, domestic work, and manual labor.

Impact of Slavery on Underdeveloped Nations:
Slavery has had a significant impact on underdeveloped nations, both in the past and present. In the past, the transatlantic slave trade devastated African societies, with millions of people

forcibly removed from their homes and forced to work in brutal conditions. The slave trade disrupted families and communities and left a lasting legacy of poverty and inequality.

Today, slavery continues to have a significant impact on underdeveloped nations. Slavery perpetuates poverty and inequality by keeping people trapped in a cycle of debt and exploitation. Slaves often work in dangerous and unhealthy conditions, which can lead to injury or illness. Slavery also contributes to environmental degradation, as industries such as mining and agriculture often have a devastating impact on the environment.

In conclusion, slavery has been a global phenomenon throughout history, and it still exists in many underdeveloped nations today. The forms of slavery vary, but debt bondage, forced labor, and human trafficking are the most common. Slavery has had a significant impact on underdeveloped nations, perpetuating poverty, inequality, and environmental degradation. It is essential to continue working to end slavery and address the root causes that allow it to persist.

Chapter XI
Colonial Exploitation of Natural Resources

Historical Overview of Colonialism:

Colonialism refers to the policy of a foreign power extending its control over a territory, typically for economic and political reasons. The colonial period lasted from the 15th to the 20th century, during which European nations, such as Britain, France, Portugal, and Spain, established colonies and empires across the Americas, Africa, and Asia. The main motive behind colonialism was to exploit the resources of the colonies to fuel the economic growth and prosperity of the colonizing nations.

Forms of Colonial Exploitation of Natural Resources:

Colonial powers engaged in various forms of exploitation of natural resources in their colonies. Some of these forms include:

Forced Labor: The colonizers used forced labor to extract natural resources, such as gold, diamonds, and minerals, from the colonies. This led to the exploitation of the local population, who were forced to work long hours under harsh conditions, often with no pay or very low wages.

Land Grabbing: The colonizers took control of large tracts of land in the colonies, often through force or deception. This resulted in the displacement of the local population, who were pushed off their land and deprived of their traditional means of livelihood.

Resource Extraction: The colonizers extracted natural resources, such as timber, rubber, and oil, from the colonies, often without regard for the environmental consequences or the impact on the local population.

Monopoly Control: The colonizers established monopolies over the production and sale of natural resources in their colonies, ensuring that the profits flowed back to the colonizing nation.

Impact of Colonial Exploitation of Natural Resources on Underdeveloped Nations/Third World:

The impact of colonial exploitation of natural resources on underdeveloped nations or third world countries was profound and far-reaching. Some of the impacts include:

Economic Exploitation: Colonial exploitation of natural resources led to the economic exploitation of underdeveloped nations, as their resources were taken away by the colonizers without any compensation or benefits.

Environmental Degradation: The extraction of natural resources by the colonizers often led to environmental degradation, as forests were cleared, rivers polluted, and ecosystems destroyed.

Social Disruption: The displacement of local populations and the use of forced labor by the colonizers led to social disruption in underdeveloped nations, as communities were torn apart, families separated, and traditional ways of life destroyed.

Political Instability: Colonialism also led to political instability in underdeveloped nations, as the colonizers often imposed their own political systems and structures on the colonies, resulting in conflict and resistance.

In conclusion, colonial exploitation of natural resources had a profound impact on underdeveloped nations and third world countries, contributing to their underdevelopment and poverty. While colonialism has officially ended, its legacy still lingers in many parts of the world, with many of these nations struggling to overcome the legacy of exploitation and oppression.

Chapter XII
Relationship between Slavery and Colonial Exploitation of Natural Resources

The relationship between slavery and colonial exploitation of natural resources has a long and complex history. European colonial powers, such as Portugal, Spain, France, the Netherlands, and Britain, established slave trade networks and used enslaved Africans to extract natural resources, such as gold, silver, cotton, tobacco, sugar, and coffee, from their colonies in the Americas, Africa, and Asia.

The transatlantic slave trade, which lasted from the 16th to the 19th century, was a massive and brutal system of forced labor that involved the kidnapping, transportation, and enslavement of millions of Africans to work on plantations and mines in the New World. The slave trade was driven by the demand for labor in the burgeoning colonial economies, which were dependent on the extraction and export of natural resources.

The relationship between slavery and colonial exploitation of natural resources took various forms, depending on the specific context and resources involved. In some cases, slaves were used to extract and process raw materials, such as gold in Brazil, silver in Mexico, and diamonds in South Africa. In other cases, slaves were used to cultivate cash crops, such as tobacco, cotton, and sugar, on plantations in the Caribbean, Brazil, and the southern United States. Slaves were also employed in the production of luxury goods, such as coffee and chocolate, in colonies in Africa and South America.

The impact of the relationship between slavery and colonial exploitation of natural resources on underdeveloped nations was profound and enduring. The extraction of resources through forced labor and colonial domination resulted in the impoverishment and underdevelopment of many regions. The slave trade disrupted local economies, cultures, and societies, as millions of people were forcibly taken from their homes and transported across the Atlantic. The use of slave labor also undermined the development of free labor markets and led to the perpetuation of poverty and inequality.

Moreover, the legacy of colonial exploitation continues to shape global economic relations today. Many former colonial powers continue to extract natural resources from former colonies through unequal trade relations and exploitative practices, such as resource extraction and land grabbing. The relationship between slavery and colonial exploitation of natural resources highlights the ongoing need for reparations, restorative justice, and the recognition of the historical and ongoing harms of colonialism and slavery.

Chapter XIII
Efforts to Address Slavery and Colonial Exploitation of Natural Resources in Underdeveloped Nations

Slavery and colonial exploitation of natural resources have been a persistent problem in many underdeveloped nations for centuries. The legacy of these practices has had a lasting impact on the economic, social, and political development of these nations. However, there have been efforts to address these issues at the international, national, and community levels.

International Efforts:

The international community has made significant efforts to address slavery and colonial exploitation of natural resources in underdeveloped nations. One of the most notable international efforts has been the establishment of the United Nations (UN) Guiding Principles on Business and Human Rights.

These principles provide a framework for businesses to respect human rights and to address any negative impacts they may have on the environment and society. The UN has also established the International Labour Organization (ILO) to promote decent working conditions, including the eradication of forced labor and child labor.

Another international initiative aimed at addressing slavery and colonial exploitation of natural resources is the Kimberley Process Certification Scheme (KPCS). The KPCS is a joint initiative between governments, industry, and civil society to prevent the trade in conflict diamonds, which are often associated with human rights abuses.

National Efforts:

Many nations have also taken steps to address slavery and colonial exploitation of natural resources within their borders. For example, some countries have implemented laws and regulations to prohibit the use of forced labor and to ensure that workers are paid fair wages. Other countries have established national parks and protected areas to conserve natural resources and prevent their exploitation.

Community Efforts:

At the community level, there have been efforts to address slavery and colonial exploitation of natural resources through activism and awareness-raising campaigns. Grassroots organizations have been formed to promote fair labor practices, environmental conservation, and sustainable development. Some of these organizations work directly with local communities to provide education and training on sustainable farming practices, renewable energy, and other alternative livelihoods.

In conclusion, while slavery and colonial exploitation of natural resources remain significant challenges in many underdeveloped nations, there have been efforts at the international, national, and community levels to address these issues. Continued collaboration and cooperation between governments, businesses, civil society, and local communities are essential to ensure that these efforts are effective and sustainable.

Chapter XIV
Conclusion

The legacy of colonialism and imperialism has had a profound impact on the world we live in today. The exploitation, oppression, and violence that characterized these historical systems of power continue to shape global politics, economics, and culture. While there have been efforts to address the injustices of colonialism and imperialism, there is still much work to be done.

In this essay, we have examined the ways in which colonialism and imperialism have influenced contemporary global relations. We have explored the origins and nature of colonialism, from the Spanish conquest of the Americas to the scramble for Africa in the late 19th century. We have also examined imperialism, which refers to the economic and political domination of one country over another, and the ways in which it has been used to exploit and oppress people around the world.

One of the key themes that emerged from our discussion is the impact of colonialism and imperialism on the economic and social development of colonized countries. The extraction of resources, forced labor, and the destruction of traditional economic systems left many countries in a state of underdevelopment that continues to this day. We also explored the impact of colonialism on culture and identity, including the imposition of European languages and religions, the erasure of indigenous cultures and knowledge systems, and the use of violence and coercion to enforce colonial rule.

Another important theme that emerged from our analysis is the role of resistance and agency in challenging colonialism and imperialism. We discussed the ways in which colonized peoples have resisted colonial domination, from armed uprisings to non-violent protests and intellectual critiques. We also examined the importance of solidarity between different struggles against colonialism and imperialism, including anti-racist and anti-capitalist movements.

Finally, we emphasized the need for continued analysis and action in addressing the legacy of colonialism and imperialism. While some progress has been made in addressing the injustices of the past, there is still much work to be done to address the ongoing impact of these systems of power. This includes addressing ongoing economic exploitation and political domination, promoting cultural and linguistic diversity, and supporting struggles for social and economic justice around the world.

In conclusion, the legacy of colonialism and imperialism is complex and multifaceted, and its impact continues to be felt in the world today. However, by understanding and analyzing the historical roots and contemporary manifestations of

these systems of power, we can work towards
building a more just and equitable global society.
This requires ongoing critical engagement,
solidarity, and action, and a commitment to
promoting social, economic, and cultural diversity
and equality.

REFERENCES

Fanon, F. (1963). The Wretched of the Earth. Grove Press.

Achebe, C. (1958). Things Fall Apart. Heinemann.

Quijano, A. (2000). Coloniality of Power, Eurocentrism, and Latin America. Nepantla: Views from South, 1(3), 533-580.
Said, E. W. (1978). Orientalism. Vintage.

Chakrabarty, D. (1992). Postcoloniality and the Artifice of History: Who Speaks for 'Indian' Pasts? Representations, 37(1), 1-26.

Du Bois, W. E. B. (1903). The Souls of Black Folk. A.C. McClurg.

Gilroy, P. (1993). The Black Atlantic: Modernity and Double Consciousness. Verso.

Wallerstein, I. (2004). World-Systems Analysis: An Introduction. Duke University Press.

Anderson, B. (1991). Imagined Communities: Reflections on the Origin and Spread of Nationalism. Verso.
Stoler, A. L. (2002). Carnal Knowledge and

Imperial Power: Race and the Intimate in Colonial Rule. University of California Press.

United Nations Guiding Principles on Business and Human Rights: https://www.ohchr.org/en/professionalinterest/pages/businessandhumanrights.aspx

International Labour Organization: https://www.ilo.org/global/lang--en/index.htm

Kimberley Process Certification Scheme: https://www.kimberleyprocess.com/

International Labour Organization Forced Labour Convention, 1930 (No. 29): https://www.ilo.org/dyn/normlex/en/f?p=NORML EXPUB:12100:0::NO::P12100_ILO_CODE:C029

International Labour Organization Minimum Wage Fixing Convention, 1970 (No. 131): https://www.ilo.org/dyn/normlex/en/f?p=NORML EXPUB:12100:0::NO::P12100_ILO_CODE:C131

The Global Slavery Index: https://www.globalslaveryindex.org/
International Institute for Sustainable Development: https://www.iisd.org/
International Union for Conservation of Nature: https://www.iucn.org/